A Writer's Dictionary of Distinctions

by
Scott K. Andersen

Second Edition

Tox Publications

Also by Scott K. Andersen:

40 Tricks with a Hot Rod
(Scott K. Anderson)
D. Robbins & Co. Inc.

Being Magic
Tox Publications

Table of Contents

Introduction

While the English language evolves for many legitimate reasons, like new technology and catch-words-of-the-day, the biggest problem with the English language is that it forgives too easily. When our words are misused, it seems it's just easier to let them be twisted enough so they encompass their incorrect usage, so they appear to be correct even when they are wrong.

It seems it's easier to change the intent of our words than it is to learn the words as they were given to us.

Perhaps there is something wrong with that.

That's why this dictionary was written – to help you eliminate from your language common errors that weaken your writing. Using the correct word at the proper moment adds power to your efforts.

We used the latest editions of leading dictionaries and standard grammar guides to confirm our usage of each word in this book. Some sources made allowances for the misused definitions. Other sources made references to the nonconformities, but were careful to indicate they were disputed. Some of the words we've listed were not even included in every dictionary.

Regardless, the definitions on the following pages are accurate and correctly express the most powerful and effective ways to use these common words. What we present here represents the best definitions, the best distinctions, and you will never be wrong in using them as we suggest.

Use them as we've noted, and your mastery of the language will only strengthen.

Some of these distinctions are quite subtle, and you might find it difficult to incorporate the proper uses of these words into your writing – it's hard to break bad habits. But read *A Writer's Dictionary of Distinctions*, become familiar with the words it covers, and use it as a reference tool every time you put the proverbial pen to paper. Before long, the proper uses of these words will be as second nature to you as the improper uses of some of them probably already are.

Embrace our language – study it, master it, explore it – make it distinctively yours.

There is no time *12:00 a.m.* or *12:00 p.m.*

Use **noon** or **midnight**. The abbreviations, a.m. and p.m., mean ante meridian and post meridian, respectively. Ante meridian means before noon, and post meridian means after noon. When it *is* noon (or midnight) you cannot *at the same time* be before or after noon – thus, the a.m. and p.m. references are wrong in those cases. (The preferred abbreviations are "a.m." and "p.m.")

Adequate does not mean *abundant*

Something that is sufficient is **adequate**: An adequate lunch for me is just two slices of pepperoni pizza.

Something that is **abundant** is plentiful: We have five rolls of toilet paper, an abundant supply for our weekend camping trip.

No admission does not mean *no admittance*

No admission means you must pay a fee to get inside.

No admittance means you need permission get inside.

Advance forward

Redundant: Anything that **advances** is already going forward.

An *adventure* is not a *quest*

Adventures are unusual and exciting experiences: Our trip through the jungle was an adventure.

Quests are searches: I am on a quest to find my blue sock.

Aggravate does not mean *irritate*

Aggravate is to increase the gravity (seriousness) of something: The way you sit aggravates your back problem.

Irritate is to annoy or make angry: The way you drive irritates me and my dog.

Alibi does not mean *excuse*

Alibi refers to claims that a person was somewhere else when a crime was committed: Her alibi was that she was washing her hair when the canary next door was killed.

Excuse means to make an apology for or to try and remove blame from: His excuse for being late was that he did not hear his alarm clock.

Allude does not mean *elude*

Allude means to refer to something: Jonathon alluded to David's letter of Nov. 11, 1981.

Elude means to escape from danger, difficulty, or a partner: I have eluded the monster.

Allude does not mean *mention*

Allude means to refer to something: I am alluding to the previous distinction.

Mention means to briefly refer to something, to specify: I also mentioned the smashed guitar to the insurance company.

Alone by itself

Redundant: If something is **alone**, it is obviously by itself.

Alot is not a word

A lot is what you should write.

Already does not mean prepared

Already means before the time in question or as soon as this: Before you called, I already knew you weren't coming.

All ready means prepared: We are all ready for our trip.

Alright is not all right

Alright should be written as two words: **all right**.

Other *alternative*

Redundant: The **alternative** is always the other.

Altogether does not mean assembled

Altogether means entirely: You are altogether wrong.

All together refers to things or persons that have been assembled: The chairs are all together in the room.

An goes before vowel sounds; *a* goes before consonant sounds

The key is sounds. Some examples: A large cat. An elephant. An SASE (self-addressed, stamped envelope) is correct because the first *sound* is the vowel "e" in the letter "s." An honest man is correct because the first *sound* in "honest" is an "o."

Angry with vs. *angry at*

You are **angry with** people and **angry at** situations: I am angry with Jackie for pushing me. I am angry at the mall for closing so early.

There are no first *annual* events

Annual means happening every year. When an event occurs for the first time, it has not yet happened *every* year: This is our first antique truck show. This is our second annual festival of cats.

Anticipate does not mean *expect*

Anticipate means to deal with or use before the proper time: I anticipated her kiss and kissed her first.

Expect means to assume as a future occurrence: I expected she would kiss me after the movie.

Old *antique*

Redundant: All **antiques** are old.

Anxious does not mean *eager*

Anxious means troubled or uneasy in the mind: I anxiously waited for my medical results.

Eager means full of desire or enthusiastic: I eagerly waited for my wife's plane to land.

Anyone? Any one? Anybody?

These are very subtle distinctions. **Anyone** refers to any person, regardless of who the person is: Is there anyone in this room I can trust?

Any one refers to a single person or thing: Can any one of those cats sing?

Anybody typically refers to someone of note, like a famous person: No one who was anybody missed the party.

Ascend upward

Redundant: To **ascend** means to move upward.

Assembled together

Redundant: When things are **assembled,** by definition they are brought together.

Audible to the ear

Redundant: Anything **audible** is such only to the ear.

Her avocation is not her career

An **avocation** is someone's minor occupation, like a hobby: Writing poetry is my avocation.

A person's major occupation is his **career**: Writing for the newspaper is my career.

To *avoid* a situation is not to *avert* it

Avoid is to keep away or refrain from something: I avoided Robby all day.

Avert is to turn away from or prevent: I averted my eyes when I saw Susan.

Awhile is one word

Awhile means for a short time.

There are no backyard *barbeques*

Barbecue is the right word for a meal cooked outside on an open flame.

Becareful is not a word

The key word is **careful**: Be careful not to strain your back.

Reason is *because*

Redundant: Because means for the reason that. Say: I was early because traffic moved quickly. Don't say: The reason I was early is because traffic moved quickly.

First *begin*

Redundant: The first thing you can ever do is **begin**.

Don't always *believe plausible* excuses

Something **plausible** seems reasonable, probable: She had a plausible excuse for coming home so late – she met a cute guy.

Believe means accepted as truth: I believe he ran over the dog because there was fur on his tires.

Between should not be used for *among*

When only two are involved, use **between**: Between you and me, we have enough money.

When more than two are involved, **among** is correct: Among the four of us, no one had any cash.

Between each

Redundant: Just use **between**: I eat candy between meals.

Biography of his life

Redundant: All **biographies** are of someone's life.

Accidents should not be *blamed on* people

Don't say: Please don't blame it on me. Instead say: Please don't **blame** me **for** the accident. Please don't **blame** me.

Men do not have *blonde* hair

Women have **blonde** hair. Men have **blond** hair.

Blowed is not a word

Blow, blew, blown are the proper tenses of the verb to blow: The wind blew down the tree. Of course, poetic license allows the use of **blowed** in creative dialogue.

Brang and *brung* are not words

Don't ever use **brang** or **brung** unless you are using poetic license in your dialogue. **Bring, brought, brought** are the proper tenses of the verb to bring: Since you brought me a gift yesterday, I am happy today.

Men do not have *brunette* hair

Men have **brunet** hair, although the reference is seldom used today. Women have **brunette** hair.

Busted does not mean to break

Bust, burst, burst are the proper tenses of the verb to break: The balloon burst when the bird landed on it.

Colloquial English allows the use of **busted** when used to mean arrested: Billy Bob is in jail after he was busted yesterday afternoon.

Can does not mean *may*

Can is to be able to do something: I can juggle.

May is to express the possibility of being able to do something or to seek permission: I may be able to eat another doughnut.

Can not is not correct

Use **cannot**. No more explanation is necessary.

Cautious does not mean *wary*

Cautious means careful: He walked cautiously on the ice.

Wary means being on your guard: I was wary of that woman's big, hairy dog.

Claim should not be used for *statement* or *allege*

Claim, among many other things, means to demand something as your due property or to submit a request for payment: I claim that dog.

Statement refers to something stated, like an account, declaration, or assertion: According to his statement, he bumped his head before falling.

Allege speaks to declaring something without proof: She alleged I brushed her hair.

Do not confuse *climatic* with *climactic*

Climatic refers to weather conditions: Significant climatic change could kill my daisies.

Climactic speaks to a climax, the event or point of greatest intensity or interest: In a thrilling climactic scene, the poodle appeared.

Clumb is not a word

The tenses of the verb to climb are **climb, climbed, climbed**: I have climbed 12 flights of stairs.

Combine into one

Redundant: To **combine** anything means to make it one.

To *confer* with someone is not to get advice

To **confer** with someone is to discuss an issue: I conferred with my wife about our spending habits.

To **counsel** someone is to give advice: I appreciate your counsel during my contract negotiations.

A man can never be your *confidante*

A man can be your **confidant**. A woman is your **confidante**.

Consensus of opinion

Redundant: A **consensus** means a general agreement of opinions.

Things that happen *continually* do not happen *continuously*

Continually means to happen frequently: My baggy pants continually slip down.

Continuously means unbroken or uninterrupted: I sat in my rocking chair continuously from noon to midnight.

Continue on

Redundant: When something **continues**, it obviously goes on.

Convey back

Redundant: **Convey** means to communicate or carry; the "back" is not necessary.

Something *credulous* is not believable

Credulous means gullible: The credulous boy traded his cow for stupid "magic" beans.

Credible means believable: The little boy is not a credible witness.

Cross over

Redundant: When you **cross** something, like a bridge, you go over it.

Cyan in color

Redundant: To say it is **cyan** (or any color) is enough.

Definite does not mean *definitive*

Something **definite** has exact, defined limits: I will definitely see you at 12:30 p.m. on Friday.

Definitive refers to something being a final, authoritative decision: The definitive ruling of the council is that you may not build your house next to mine.

Point of *destination*

Redundant: Your **destination** is the point where you are going.

Differ does not mean *disagree*

Differ refers to things that are unlike others, distinguishable: His hat differs from mine.

Disagree refers to people who hold different opinions: She disagreed with me about the saltiness of the fries.

Dilemma does not mean problem

A **dilemma** is where you have a choice between two equally undesirable alternatives: My dilemma was that I could go out with Bob or stay home with Ron.

To *disagree* is not to *contradict*

When people **disagree**, they have different opinions about an issue: I disagreed with her about how fast we were allowed to go.

When people **contradict** each other, they deny or express the opposite of a statement: The balls were dark green; she contradicted me when she said they were dark blue.

Disgust does not mean *displease*

Disgust is a strong aversion to something, repugnance: I am finally disgusted with broccoli.

Displease is to annoy, offend: Her squeaky voice displeased me.

Disinterested does not mean *uninterested*

Disinterested means not influenced by something: Though I work for Volvo, I am disinterested from buying a Volvo car.

Uninterested means not interested: I am uninterested in zoos.

Disregardless is not a word

Disregard means to pay no attention to: He disregarded me after I kissed him.

Divide up

Redundant: **Divide** is sufficient.

Something _doublechecked_ was not checked

Double-check is correct: I wasn't sure I won the lottery until I double-checked my ticket.

Drawed is not a word

The tenses of the verb to draw are **draw, drew, drawn**: I drew the winning number. The winning number was drawn at midnight.

Slow _drawl_

Redundant: A **drawl** is slow by definition.

Drink up

Redundant: Use **drink** by itself. When making a toast, you **drink to** something.

He was not _drugged_ through the mud

The tenses of the verb to drag are **drag, dragged, dragged**: The horse dragged him through the field.

Each and every one

Redundant: Say **each one** or **every one**.

Each other vs. *one another*

When only two are involved, use **each other**: Jack and John hugged each other.

When three or more are involved, use **one another**: The three of us slapped one another on our backs after we won the game.

Fear does not *effect* the mind

Affect means to influence something: The music may affect our mood tonight.

Effect means the result of something: The effects of the wreck were devastating. **Effect** also means to accomplish: The new boss will effect many changes.

Scandalous affairs are not *elicit*

Elicit is to evoke or draw out a response or an admission: His remarks elicited a blow to his nose.

Illicit is something unlawful or forbidden: Cocaine is an illicit substance.

Enormity does not mean large size

Enormity means extreme wickedness: The enormity of the witch's spell caused me to lose my eyes.

Try **enormous** for large size: He had an enormous stomach last summer.

Enthuse is not an accepted word

Enthuse is mistakenly used for the word **enthusiastic**, which means showing strong interest: He was not as enthusiastic about the clowder of cats as she was.

Dinner is not an *essential* meal

Something that is **essential** is absolutely necessary: Fire is essential for barbecue cooking.

Everyone vs. *every one*

Everyone refers to all people and takes the singular verb: Everyone loves my book.

Every one refers to each individual item or person: Every one of the mice nibbled on the cheese.

Evoke is not to call upon a higher power

To **evoke** is to inspire emotions or memories: The song on the radio evoked memories of our last summer together.

To **invoke** is to call on a deity in prayer, to petition for help or support: He invoked the god tox when he prayed.

Something *exceptional* is not always *objectionable*

Something **exceptional** is unusual, not typical: What an exceptional dancing dog that is.

Something **exceptionable** is open to objection: Your tardiness is based on exceptionable circumstances.

Something **objectionable** is unpleasant, offensive: He has objectionable foot odor.

To *explain* is not to *elucidate*

To **explain** is to make clear with details: He explained the game's rules to me several times.

To **elucidate** is to throw light on something: The manager's report elucidated our situation.

True *fact*

Redundant: Something that is a **fact** is by nature true.

Good meals are not *fantastic*

Fantastic comes from the word fantasy and means something extravagantly fanciful, eccentric: Michael Jackson's home was probably fantastic.

Farce does not mean *mockery*

A **farce** is something that is ludicrously impossible: The idea that my mother and your grandfather danced nude together is a farce.

Mockery is to ridicule: That story makes a mockery of your father.

Farther vs. *further*

Farther refers to measurable distances: I can run one mile farther.

Further means in addition, going to a greater extent: Let us talk about the matter further before deciding.

A woman can never be a *fiancé*

Men are **fiancés**; women are **fiancées**. Both are persons engaged to be married, and both words are pronounced the same way.

You should not *fix* a broken engine

While it is true that **fix** is commonly used in this context, **repair** is a stronger word. While there are numerous definitions for **fix**, one of its strongest is to make firm or stable: When the paint dried, my hair was fixed to the wall.

Flout does not mean making a show of

To **flout** is to express contempt: I get annoyed when you flout my rules like that.

Flaunt is to make a show of, display ostentatiously: She flaunted her fancy hat all night long.

You *follow up* on the *follow-up*

Follow up is a verb meaning to continue and complete an action: I need to follow up on our conversation yesterday.

Follow-up is a noun and adjective meaning anything that follows something else as a review, addition: Our follow-up conversation was a waste of time.

Free *gift*

Redundant: All **gifts** are free or they are not gifts.

Gratuitous does not mean done for *appreciation*

Something **gratuitous** refers to things that are done free of charge, uncalled for: My mechanic gratuitously rotated my tires.

Something done in **appreciation** is done for recognition: I was given a gold bar in appreciation of my daily showers.

A **gratuity** is money given in recognition of service.

Unless you are British, use *gray*, not *grey*

While both spellings of the color are correct, **gray** is considered the American version; **grey** is the United Kingdom version. (Remember "a" in "gray" for "America.")

Half-staff is not *half-mast*

Flags are flown at **half-staff** or **half-mast** to show respect, mourning, or distress. To say a flag is at "half-mast" refers to flags flown on ships. (Ships have masts.) Otherwise, the flag is being flown at half-staff.

There are no *healthy* foods

Healthful is something that is conducive to good health: Eat some healthful carrots today.

Healthy refers to something in good health: Because they exercise, we have healthy children.

Something *historical* is not always famous in history

Something of or concerning history is **historical**: These are historical shoes, the ones Ben wore in the big game.

Something that is famous in history is **historic**: This flag marks the historic battle that liberated the zoo.

Convicted killers are never *hung* to death

Objects are **hung**; people are **hanged**: After the curtains were hung in place, the murderer was hanged to death.

I.E. does not mean "for example"

I.E. means "in other words": The industry is getting weak, i.e., your products will not sell well next year.

E.G. means "for example": We need 16 furry animals, e.g., cats, dogs, raccoons, or hamsters.

Same *identical*

Redundant: If it's **identical**, it is already the same.

Don't use *if* and *when* together

If means there is a chance you will do something, while **when** means you will do that something. They negate each other when used together.

Illusion does not mean reference

An **illusion** is something that is deceptive: Her small appetite is an illusion – she is really starving.

An **allusion** is a reference to something: Her allusion to Stephen King's speech made her appearance more meaningful for me.

Implying something does not *infer* it

To **imply** something is to strongly suggest its existence or that it is true: He implied he had bought me a broom for Christmas.

Infer is to deduce or conclude from facts: Because of the used litter box, I inferred there was cat in the house.

Now *in progress*

Redundant: Anything **in progress** is happening now.

Incredulous does not mean *unbelievable*

Incredulous means unwilling to believe: It is, of course, an incredulous claim to make, that you jumped from here to there.

Unbelievable means not believable: I just read an unbelievable story about cats petting dogs.

Present *incumbent*

Redundant: An **incumbent** is someone who presently holds a position.

Infectious is not necessarily *contagious*

Contagious diseases are transmitted by contact: Warts are a contagious disease.

Infectious diseases can be transmitted by air or water: The common cold is an infectious disease.

Something *inflammable* is *flammable*

Inflammable and **flammable** both mean combustible.

Non-flammable refers to something that cannot be set on fire.

Natural *instinct*

Redundant: **Instinct** is natural, by definition.

Practice does not *insure* mastery

Insure means something relating to a *written* contract or insurance policy: My contract insures I will make $100 profit.

Ensure means to make certain: The boss ensured the recommendations were implemented.

First *introductions*

Redundant: **Introductions** are always first.

Irregardless is not a word

Use **regardless** without the "ir." Regardless means without consideration for: He walked on the lawn regardless of the snakes.

It's means it is; *its* is the possessive

Learn this well. **It's** means it is: It's odd that you are so late.

Its is the possessive of "it": Its fleas jumped on me.

Joined together

Redundant: When things are **joined**, they are brought together.

The *latest* thing is not the *last* thing

The **latest** thing is the most recent item in an ongoing series: His fourth book is his latest; he has begun his fifth.

The **last** thing is the final one: This is the last of the hot dogs.

Old *legend*

Redundant: All **legends** are old.

If you can count them, do not use *less*

Use **fewer** with objects that can easily be counted: Fewer books were sold today than yesterday.

Use **less** when referring to things not easily counted, like amounts, degrees, or value: We need less criticism from our employees.

Livid should not be used for *enraged*

Livid refers to things that are discolored, like by a bruise: His livid face revealed he was a boxer.

Enraged is to make furious: My neighbor's loud music enraged everyone in the house.

You do not *loan* money

Loan is a noun: The money she gave me was a loan.

Lend is a verb: Will you lend me your umbrella?

Mad does not mean *angry*

Mad means insane: Her cat's snoring drove her mad.

Angry means extremely displeased or resentful: I was angry with Frank when he wrecked my tricycle.

Not all elected officials win by a *majority* of the vote

Majority means more than half: The majority of the people polled agree with Cindy.

Plurality means the highest number within a greater number. If three people ran for office and the first received 40 percent of the votes, the second received 39 percent, and the third received 21 percent, the first candidate won by a plurality.

Matinee in the afternoon

Redundant: All **matinees** are in the afternoon.

Complete *monopoly*

Redundant: A **monopoly** is complete control.

Morale does not refer to a lesson

Morale refers to the mental balance of a person or a group: The workers' morale was low after the strike.

Moral refers to something concerned with the goodness or badness of a human, the lesson of a story: The counselor exhibited what we considered to be good, moral behavior when around the children.

Mutual does not mean *common*

Mutual means reciprocally exchanged, having the same relationship: The mutual devotion between herself and the cat was unexpected.

Common refers to something shared equally: We held a common belief in green dogs.

Nine in number

Redundant: There is no reason to say that **nine** (or any number) is a number. Just say "nine" (or whatever the number is).

Fictitious *novel*

Redundant: By definition, all **novels** are works of fiction.

Older and *elder* are slightly different

Both **older** and **elder** refer to people, but **older** also refers to things. Examples: The older chair is my favorite one. The elder man won the race.

Opposites are not *incomparable*

Something **incomparable** is without an equal: For an incomparable hole in the ground, check out the Grand Canyon.

Something **opposite** is diametrically (completely) different: We have opposite views on abortion.

Parameter does not mean limit

Parameter is a characteristic or feature: A parameter of this job includes unloading the truck.

Perimeter is the outer limit of an area: The dog ran to the perimeter of the yard and barked like a maniac all night.

Something *particular* is not *specific*

Particular things are distinct from other things: He paints with a particular style.

Specific things are clearly defined: Red, sharp lines describe his specific painting style.

Usually, *party* does not mean *person*

A **party** is a person or persons forming one side of an agreement or a dispute: I am now a party in your lawsuit.

Use **person** in all other cases involving humans: The first person I spoke with spit on me.

Individual *person*

Redundant: Every **person** is an individual.

The plural of *person* is not *people*

The plural of **person** is persons: Several persons came into the shop today.

The word **people** refers to persons comprising a group, community, race, etc.: Those neighborhood people who planned the show did a good job.

Advanced *planning*

Redundant: All **planning** is done in advance.

Possible things are not always *probable*

Possible things are capable of existing or happening: A possible solution is just to remember my birthday.

Probable things are expected to happen: A probable scenario is we will get a Christmas bonus.

Practicable plans are not always *practical*

Practicable refers to something that can be done or used: He gave us a practicable plan for crossing the river.

Practical refers to something suited to practice or use: Spatulas are practical tools for flipping pancakes.

Precede does not mean continue

Precede means to come or go before something, or to be ahead of or in front of something: The letter "Q" precedes the letter "V."

Proceed means to continue, move along: The puppy proudly proceeded down the path.

Pristine does not mean spotless

Pristine means in its original condition: I lost the unopened and pristine deck of playing cards.

"To be or not to be" is not a *quote*

Quote is a verb: Let me quote Shakespeare for you.

Quotation is a noun: "To be or not to be" is a famous quotation.

Children are not *raised*

Children are **reared**: She reared three children by herself.

Animals and plants are **raised**: He raised beets one summer.

Rarely ever

Redundant: Things that **rarely** happen rarely ever happen.

Refute does not mean *repudiate* or *deny*

Refute means to prove a falsity or error of a statement: He refuted the accuracy of my budget numbers.

Repudiate means to disown, disavow, or reject: He repudiated me after I changed my name.

Deny is to declare untrue: He denied the dog's existence.

Regrettable does not mean *sorrowful* or *regret*

Regrettable means undesirable and unwelcome: The spider my brother gave me for Christmas was a regrettable gift.

Sorrowful means full of sorrow: The dog had dark, sorrowful eyes.

Regret is to feel or express sorrow: I regret hanging up on my mother last night.

Repeat again

Redundant: When something is **repeated**, it is done again.

End *result*

Redundant: **Results** are always at the end of something.

Revelry is not a morning bugle call

Revelry means to have a good time: At midnight, our revelry got out of hand.

Reveille is when military personnel are awakened: Reveille sounds at 4:00 a.m., gosh.

Revert back

Redundant: To **revert** means to go back to an earlier state.

Mechanical _robot_

Redundant: All **robots** are mechanical.

Rumors are not necessarily _lies_

A **rumor** is an unfounded or unverified story: Rumors of my bankruptcy are rather premature.

Lies are untruths: You lied when you said I stole your cookies.

Scarce things are not _rare_

Something **scarce** is insufficient for demand: Water was scarce after the fire.

Something **rare** is seldom done or found: Three-legged chickens are rare.

Seldom ever

Redundant: The word **seldom** by itself is sufficient.

You must *set up* the *setup*

Set up is a verb: Please set up your drums by the stairs.

Setup is a noun and adjective: The drum setup was ideal for a one-handed woman.

Silence does not mean *quiet*

Silence means absence of sound: Silence finally settles in when no one else is home.

Quiet means with little or no sound: The librarian insisted I quietly sharpen my pencil.

Snuck is not a word

Sneak, sneaked, sneaked are the proper verb tenses: The kitten sneaked away.

Somewheres is not a word

Just use **somewhere**, without the second "s," please.

Vocal *song*

Redundant: All **songs** are vocal.

It takes more than *soothing* to *appease* someone

To **soothe** someone is to calm them: He soothed her by reminding her that he loved her.

To **appease** someone is to soothe them by making concessions: I appeased the dog by opening a second can of food.

Square in shape

Redundant: There is no need to say that **square** (or rectangular, or triangular, etc.) refers to a shape. Just say "square" (or whatever shape it is).

Stack up

Redundant: To **stack** things is to stack them up.

Strait does not mean not crooked

Strait is a narrow passage of water connecting two bodies of water: The ship moved slowly through the strait.

Straight means not crooked or curved: The straight path took me to the hot dog stand.

Suburbs of the city

Redundant: All **suburbs** are of nearby cities.

Suspect changes when you *believe*

Suspect means to have an impression of the existence or presence of something: I suspected the cat was behind the curtain.

When used in the sense of **believe**, suspect means to believe *without clear reason*: Even though there was a traffic jam, I suspected he didn't come straight home.

Temporarily *suspended*

Redundant: **Suspensions** are always temporary.

Mental *telepathy*

Redundant: All **telepathy** is mental.

Theirselves is not a word

Use **themselves**: They are hurting themselves by eating so much hard candy.

Thusly is not a word

Drop the "ly" and use **thus**. Thus means in this way: I had memorized the way, thus I was able to run to the store.

'Till does not mean until

Drop the apostrophe and **till** means until. (Till, by the way, should never be used at the beginning of a sentence – use "until.")

Something *tortuous* is not painful

Tortuous means full of twists and turns, devious: The tortuous labyrinth confused us.

Torturous means painful: His torturous backrubs frighten me.

Transpire does not mean *happen*

Transpire means come to be known: What transpired was that we learned the name of the cat thief.

Happen means to occur: What happened was that the fifth cat was stolen.

Treacherous does not mean *dangerous*

Treacherous means guilty of violating faith, betraying trust: Selling my story idea without my knowledge was treacherous.

Dangerous means not safe, exposure to harm: Drinking poison is dangerous.

Honest *truth*

Redundant: The **truth** is always honest.

Two *twins*

Redundant: **Twins** always come in pairs. (Don't forget triplets, etc.)

Most *unique*

Redundant: Something **unique** cannot be most or more unique.

Usually always

Incorrect. **Usually** means often, but not all the time: I usually eat lunch at noon. **Always** means all the time: I always jog before breakfast. When used together, they negate each other.

Visible to the eye

Redundant: Anything **visible** obviously can be seen by the eye.

Lunch is not *vital*

Vital should only be used if life or continued existence is involved: Eating is vital.

Warn beforehand

Redundant: **Warnings** always come beforehand.

Rugs are not *weaved*

Weave, **wove**, **woven** are the verb tenses: The woman wove the pretty shag rug.

Weaved is correct only when something moves in a zigzag manner: The car weaved through traffic.

Well is not the same as *good*

Good is an adjective: He was a good dancer.

Well is an adverb: He danced well Friday night.

Widow woman

Redundant: All **widows** are women, just as all **widowers** are men.

Bonus Distinctions

Commas and periods always – *always* – go inside quotation marks

Despite our best efforts, we could not find any rule in American English that allows for a period or comma to go outside of quotation marks. They always go inside – *always* – even if you are using a single quotation mark. (Question marks and exclamation points are not periods and/or commas and so rely on their own usage rules.) **Examples**: "I am quoting myself." The dog barked "bowwow." "You remind me of a 'clown,'" she said.

You can't have your cake and eat it, too

Incorrect. Anyone can have a cake and eat it. You should say: **You can't eat your cake and have it, too**. (After you eat it, it's gone, so you can't also have it.) That's the way it was first written.

www.ingramcontent.com/pod-product-compliance
Lightning Source LLC
Chambersburg PA
CBHW070840290526
45795CB00002B/926